Tropical Paradise

QUEENSLAND

MAGNIFICENT PANORAMIC VIEWS

*Never get so busy making a living
that you forget to make a life.*

PANOGRAPHS®
PUBLISHING PTY LTD

Seize the day,

put no trust in tomorrow.

HORACE

Tropical North Queensland, the region north of the Tropic of Capricorn, is monsoon affected, with two defined seasons. Most tourists come in the cooler time of year, the Dry Season, which is May through to October, but one of Ken's favourite times is through the Wet Season. At this time the waterfalls are flowing or raging and the storm activity provides some great lighting opportunities.

This book includes stunning photographs from the Whitsunday Islands in the south all the way up the eastern coast to the very tip of Cape York Peninsula. Some of the islands off the coast of this region are without doubt among the most beautiful places in the world. God was certainly having a great day when He made Whitsunday and Lizard Islands, and to top it off He gave us the Great Barrier Reef – a jewel in the Earth's crown.

The rainforests of Mossman Gorge and the Daintree take you back in time to the dawn of creation – rejuvenating your soul as you meander through these ancient havens and breathe in their fresh air.

The waterfalls that are spread throughout the hinterlands have so many different characteristics that it would take many visits to the area to appreciate them all.

We hope the images in this book, taken by internationally renowned photographer Ken Duncan, will continue to inspire you if you have visited this area – and if you have not, we hope they excite you to go. Ken has a special gift to really capture the spirit of a place and is one of the major pioneers in the resurgence of panoramic photography among the new generation. It is with great pleasure that Ken shares his images from his adventures in this great region.

*Where
there is love
there is life.*

With their roots deep in rich volcanic soil,
the tree ferns of the Atherton Tablelands thrive on the
tropical rainfall that keeps innumerable waterfalls
flowing all year. The name of these beautiful falls,
Millaa Millaa, is an Aboriginal word for "plenty of
water" – and it's easy to see why.

TITLE PAGE
Whitehaven Beach, Qld

PREVIOUS PAGE
Chilli Beach, Cape York, Qld

THIS PAGE
Millaa Millaa Falls, Qld

Those who bring sunshine to the lives of others cannot keep it from themselves.

Hinchinbrook Island is a spectacular wilderness of granite mountains, impenetrable jungle and thick mangrove swamps. Here, gentle white puffs of cloud are reflected in the glassy beauty of the remote and spectacular Zoe Bay.

THIS PAGE
Zoe Bay, Hinchinbrook Island, Qld

NEXT PAGE
Palm Cove, Qld

6

*Man's heart
away from nature
becomes hard.*

*From deep within a tropical rainforest the Mossman
River flows, its waters tumbling forth from lofty
mountain heights to crystal clear ponds below.
Boulders strewn in the sparkling water make
perfect stools on which to sit and bathe
in the beauty of creation.*

Mossman Gorge, Qld

*Kind words can be short
and easy to speak,
but their echoes
are truly endless.*

Low Isles is an idyllic, unspoilt four-acre coral cay,
a jewel in the middle of the Great Barrier Reef lagoon.
A true tropical paradise, here you can lie under
a beach umbrella, slip into the water to experience
the brilliantly coloured coral gardens and the fish
which inhabit them, or stroll to the island's iconic
lighthouse for a different view.

THIS PAGE
Low Isles, Great Barrier Reef, Qld

NEXT PAGE
Noahs Beach, Cape Tribulation, Qld

13

*In wilderness I sense
the miracle of life,
and behind it our scientific
accomplishments fade
to trivia.*

Here torrents of water thunder over the majestic
Barron Falls and a cloud of mist envelopes the
surrounding rainforest. This is where the Barron River
makes its descent from the Atherton Tablelands
to the Cairns coastal plain, but the volume of water
seen here only happens after substantial rainfall
during the Wet Season.

Barron Falls, Kuranda, Qld

17

*Life can be tough
but we can be tougher.*

The sun slides into the ocean at the end
of another day at Frangipani Beach,
which is Australia's northern-most mainland beach.
This gorgeous location is named after the numerous
native frangipani trees which are scattered
along its shores.

THIS PAGE
Frangipani Beach, Cape York, Qld

NEXT PAGE
Alma Bay, Magnetic Island, Qld

*Our perspective
only changes
when we change
our position.*

*Heart Reef, a stunning composition of coral naturally
formed into the shape of a heart, is located within the
Great Barrier Reef. The blues and greens of the water,
rich like precious jewels, are best experienced from
the sky by helicopter or seaplane.*

Heart Reef, Great Barrier Reef, Qld

If you're going through hell, keep going.

These wild orange flames and gusts of black smoke might look fierce, but this is a controlled fire deliberately lit in a field of sugar cane near Airlie Beach. Cane growers burn their mature crops just before harvest to remove excess leaves, leaving the tall canes blackened and ready for cutting.

Cane fire, near Airlie Beach, Qld

The sun is up,
the sky is blue,
it's beautiful,
and so are you.

The fresh, translucent waters of Eliot Creek
roll over Fruit Bat Falls, a tropical oasis on the
Cape York Peninsula. Located amongst rugged
wilderness, these cool, refreshing falls provide
a perfect break from the dust – no crocodiles here!

Fruit Bat Falls, Cape York, Qld

Imagination is more important than knowledge. Knowledge is limited. Imagination encircles the world.

The rich green fan palms of Cape Tribulation hold their wheel-like foliage aloft to give shade from the draining tropical heat. Named in 1770 by a somewhat despondent Captain Cook after he ran aground on nearby Endeavour Reef, this area is one of Australia's richest rainforest habitats.

THIS PAGE
Fan Palms, Cape Tribulation, Qld

NEXT PAGE
Green Island, Great Barrier Reef, Qld

Love, like a river,
will cut a new path
whenever it meets
an obstacle.

Josephine Creek begins as a trickle, high on the
south-eastern side of the summit of Queensland's
highest mountain, Mount Bartle Frere. About 7.5km
from the summit, the creek's waters tumble over
granite boulders, forming the turbulent Josephine Falls
which are surrounded by mesophyll vine forest –
the most complex rainforest type in Australia.

Josephine Falls,
Wooroonooran National Park, Qld

Sunsets are so beautiful that they almost seem as if we were looking through the gates of Heaven.

The afterglow of another glorious Queensland sunset saturates Sunset Beach on Lizard Island with a divine light. This ruggedly beautiful island is a remote private paradise featuring 24 powdery white beaches, surrounded by coral reefs, ribbons and lagoon reefs teeming with marine life.

THIS PAGE
Sunset Beach, Lizard Island, Qld

NEXT PAGE
Ellis Beach, Qld

CLAUDE M. BRISTOL

*It is the constant
and determined effort
that breaks down
all resistance,
sweeps away all obstacles.*

Said to be the widest falls in Australia,
the lacy curtain of Millstream Falls forms the perfect
backdrop for this spectacular natural amphitheatre.
These rushing falls spill over an old basalt lava flow,
a legacy of the Atherton Tablelands' volcanic past.

Millstream Falls, Qld

No pessimist ever discovered the secret of the stars, or sailed to an uncharted land, or opened a new doorway for the human spirit.

A sea eagle's nest sits like a sentinel overlooking the incredible view from Lizard Island, on the magical Great Barrier Reef. This pure and pristine tropical getaway offers some of Australia's best diving opportunities.

THIS PAGE
Blue Lagoon, Lizard Island, Qld

NEXT PAGE
Langford Reef, Whitsundays, Qld

*Character
develops itself
in the stream
of life.*

The beautiful Bloomfield Falls tumble 40 metres
through the ancient World Heritage Listed Daintree
rainforest. The picturesque falls are especially
spectacular after the Wet Season, but unfortunately
swimming is not a good idea as estuarine crocodiles
inhabit the river below.

Bloomfield Falls, Qld

*Patience is the key
to paradise.*

Cool, clear aqua water laps at the rocks
which border Fantome Island, a wondrous paradise
in the Great Palm Island group, 65km north-east
of Townsville. In the background, neighbouring Palm
Island is crowned by clouds, while the brilliant
Australian sun sets this blissful scene.

Fantome Island, Qld

Hill Inlet, Whitsunday Island, Qld

DESTINATION TROPICAL PARADISE

First published 2009
by Panographs Publishing Pty Ltd
ABN 21 050 235 606
PO Box 3015 Wamberal
NSW 2260 Australia
Telephone +61 2 4367 6777
Email: panos@kenduncan.com

Panographs is a registered trademark of the Ken Duncan Group Pty Limited.
Photography & text by Ken Duncan
©2009 Divine Guidance P/L
Designed by Good Catch Design
Reprographics by CFL Print Studio
Printed and bound in China

The National Library of Australia Cataloguing-in-Publication entry:

Destination tropical paradise
Queensland: magnificent panoramic views / photographer Ken Duncan.
ISBN 9780980445398
Queensland - Pictorial works.
919.43

To view the range of Ken Duncan's panoramic Limited Edition Prints visit our Galleries:

- 414 The Entrance Road, **Erina Heights, NSW** Telephone +61 2 4367 6701
- 73 George Street, The Rocks, **Sydney, NSW** Telephone +61 2 9241 3460
- Level 1. 9 Star Circus **Harbour Town Shopping Centre Docklands, Vic** Telephone +61 3 9670 6971
- Shop 14 Hunter Valley **Gardens Village, Broke Road, Pokolbin, NSW** Telephone +61 2 4998 6711
- 63 Abbott Street **Cairns, Qld** Telephone +61 7 4051 3999